POEMS FOR PARENTS

MURIEL LETMAN

A catalogue record for this book is available from the British Library

ISBN 978-1-908318-42-8

PALACE PARK PRESS

POEMS FOR PARENTS

ADVICE TO STUCK GROWNUPS!

Illustrations by
Mariella (9), Camilla (8) & Philipp (5)

WANTED

It used to be –
before the pill –
that girls, it seemed, gave birth at will;
babies born each
year on year
were every woman's constant fear.
The swinging sixties
changed all that,
women knew
what they were at –
Every child a wanted child.

No 'accidents' or 'adoption' kids.
No more she does just as he bids,
Parenthood is undertaken
when choice is made, resolve unshaken,
(excepting Catholics and Jews, who still
have rhythmic good news without the pill).
Every child a wanted child.

With millions of abortions to get rid of
the rest –
for a wanted child is surely the best,
a woman now 'chooses' motherhood
so, as a mother she'd better be good.

The pill has removed one tyranny
but set up another anxiety…

Every mother a wanted mother.

WHAT DO I DO?

She looks so small and helpless
He sounds in such distress.

Should I pick her up?
Shall I feed him more?
Do I leave the light on?
Should I close the door?
Is she better on her tummy?
Shall I lay him on his back?
Was it three hours or four now?
Oh no! I can't keep track.
Is she crying 'cos she's hungry?
Is his cry a cry of pain?
I know I changed his nappy
Perhaps I should do it all again?

I look so very helpless.
I sound in such distress.

FARTHER TIME

It seems a long way off.
Growth and development is obviously the reason.
It will arrive in August – nine months to go.
Just in time for the next football season.

To look at us now
you can scarcely find a clue
of the miracle due to take place,
except for the confusion in my head
and the hint of a smile on her face.

We'll need more cash.

We'll need more space.

She'll give up work.
I'll increase the mortgage
(just in case).
I'll paint the spare room,
buy some toys.
Which are more expensive,
girls or boys?

It's been O.K. just her and me.
Friends & family come, but they go.
Odd to be permanently three.
Will I still be her main concern?
Time and affection must divide.

Don't think of that any more.
The main task now…
to provide.

CONCEPTION . . .
A GOOD IDEA

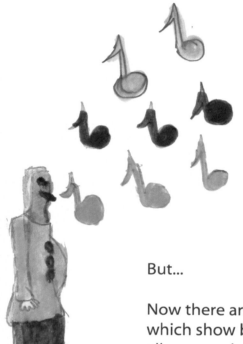

She talks to her baby.
She sings to her child
as it aimlessly floats in the
womb.
She converses and argues.
She warns and enquires
just as if it was there, in the
room.
We all think she's crazy.
The baby can't hear.
She's wasting her time,
she's a nut!

But...

Now there are scans
which show babies can smile
all wrapped up inside their cocoons.
At thirty-four weeks
they can move, blink and suck,
they'll be sending text
messages soon.

It is truly amazing
how a foetus can act
eighteen weeks sees it
wriggle and yawn.
They're researching a lot
this pre-natal adventure
which happens before we are born.

They can now scan a baby at
seven weeks gone.
The blurred images provoke
great attention.
If they go on this way, as
technology grows,
they might find it's alive at
conception.

NIGHT WATCH

Silent breathing,
fingers bent,
Sleeping gently,
heaven sent,
Mother watches
Father too…
As your parents
looked at you.

REALITY

Our lives are now child-centred,
the child has centre stage.
His name in the appointments diary
occurs on every page.
Get jabs done at the Doctors,
to the clinic to be weighed.
His parents come on Saturday
My God! How long they
stayed!
Her parents, Sunday
afternoon,
conversation never strayed –
'Ben's such a lovely baby'
'You'll need a bigger cot'
(until we had to go through
this I liked Ben quite a lot)

Our friends who have no children,
seem reluctant now to visit.
Perhaps they feel deprived
or maybe lucky – well, which is it?
The high chairs and the buggies,
the pampers and the car seats,
the sticky bibs, the baby food
he splatters as he eats.
To think we once had time to sleep
spare money we could spend.
The baby is only eight months old,
please – will it ever end!

PIN PRICK

Vaccination?
Risk assessment.
Evaluation.
Vacillation.
Sick child.
Anxious parents!
Competent medics
Vaccination…yes.

DINNER PARTY

Eat up all your dinner now,
No, no, no!

Eat the orange carrots then,
No, no, no!

Come on eat a mouthful, please,
No, no, no!

Just one little spoonful, quick,
Kick, kick, kick!

Here, one little spoonful, quick,
Spit, throw, flick!

O.K. do without your food!
Yes, yes, yes.

Mummy eat it up then?
Nod, nod, nod.

(mummy loses on both counts:
his riot and her diet)

TWO SOON...

You have achieved such skills
Mobility
Emerging speech
Self-feeding
And the battle of wills.

TWO SOON

Candles, crisps, small sausages,
a party now you're two.
Several cars, three dumper trucks,
so much given by so few.

Progressed from fettered cot
to the freedom of a bed.
The changes are so rapid,
just how two years have sped.

All those unworn bootees,
and baby-grows, size one,
now ready to be packed away
outgrown by our son.

It seems a shame to waste them,
so we look forward to next June.
As if we have not suffered enough
it has been confirmed – two soon!

DOUBLE BLESSING

One child is a treasure,
two kids are a rush.

One child sits in comfort;
in the car – two is a crush.

One child goes to bed
then the parents can relax,
but with two there is no interval
your nerves are showing cracks.

You bath them both together
to cut down on the time,
and parents just communicate
by phone or text or mime.

One child is sleeping peacefully
but the other is awake,
and we have to change the car
to fit the gear we must now take.

We've forgotten all the carefree days
when we had friends to tea.
If life's this hectic now with two,
God preserve us, please, from three!

PROGRESS

It surely is not time for that,
don't be such a fool,
we haven't had him long enough,
he can't be starting school!

Kindergarten – Nursery
call it what you like.
He'll mould the Play-doh,
play with sand, dress up or ride a bike.

He must vary his experience,
for now he's just turned four.
Liquids, solids, materials,
shapes, textures and much more.

Initial writing, painting,
some sticking things with glue,
group outings to the local park -
all these things that he must do.

He must vary his experience
of course, that's plain to see.
But what a shame he is so busy.
We just can't let him BE.

WORLD-BEATERS

Other parents
have such brilliant offspring.
Listen to them – owners of
the early walkers,
independent eaters,
fluent talkers.
All their progeny are world-beaters.

Other parents
should be more realistic,
assess their little darlings
and be less idealistic.
Release them from their ivory towers
and admit the best kids in the world
are OURS!

LETTING ME GO

Hold me!
Hold me!
Hold my hand.
I must know you understand.
I want to take my first big stride,
I can't because I'm terrified.
But I must learn to stand alone.
A fact, for me as yet unknown.
I'm washed and clothed,
observed and fed
from wake up time till I go to bed.

Hold me.
Hold me.
Hold my fingers.
The fear inside still obstinately lingers.

Please let go – I will.
No – I won't.
Just for a moment
No – please don't!

Who has the confidence
parent or child?
'I can do it' – 'he can do it'.
They both smiled.

EMERGING

How wonderful… I am five.
To be closely cared for
yet independent – moving about
running – feeding – talking – playing.
I've grasped the basics of being alive.

How interesting seems the world.
Colours – sounds – textures – shapes to be explored.
Plants – vehicles – clothes – creatures – stories
daily mysteries to be unfurled.

Yet how tragic to be just four plus one
restricted on all sides.
Hurry up – come on – stop it – put it away
wear the blue one – in the car.
When can I choose, not ordered to get it done?

Life is such a confusing mix.
Perhaps it will be better when I'm six.

GRANDSON

Grandma had a little boy.

That boy is now my Dad.

She says she loves me twice as much.

The son of the son she had.

THOUGHTS OF A GRANDMA...

The grandchildren carry life on,
they offer a further dimension
and indicate future potential
to be revealed long after I've gone.

What a pleasure to care for a grandchild,
to watch as she plays in the bath,
or digs up the worms in the garden
and watch the facial expressions
as they struggle, achieve and then laugh.

Parents are often too busy
for stories or puzzles or rhymes,
but Grandma's life is less pressurized
So she has the blessing of time.
Time for the blossom or conkers,
exploration of snow or rainwater.
Time to view holiday photos
with an excited grandson or granddaughter.

Parents are rushing and coping,
trying to keep things on track.
Grandma enjoys every moment.
When she doesn't –
She just hands them back!

WHICH SCHOOL?

Day School? Boarding? Formal? Free?
Which one is it going to be?
The one that she can walk to…?
A church school I'd prefer…
At private school he'd meet our sort…
We must now face the issue, don't defer
another hour, but study the prospectus,
league tables and school report.

A cosmopolitan atmosphere
will broaden out their view.
But why face a barrage of confused ideas
every experience something new?
They need to acquire our own culture
so they know all the things that we know.
The school is the fertile allotment
where the seeds of the nation grow.

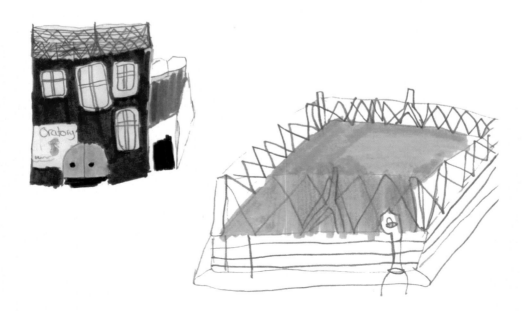

It is desperately important
to access the best schools.
But selection is such a lottery,
there are such rigid rules.
We may have to move our home,
despite the years of deep attachment,
so we can satisfy the powers that
we're in the appropriate catchment.

We've donated electronic gear
and helped out with the sports,
assured them we're reliable
exactly the right sort.
We've sent in all the references
and ended all the fuss.
We've made our careful choice of school…
But will they now choose us?

To playground

IN THE BATH AT SIX

The drips slowly slide
down the shiny white
mountainside,
merge into the still blue lake.

My toes agitate the surface to make
it into an angry crashing ocean.
Sea craft are thrashing wildly,
some sink, others float.
I cast the wrecks to their doom,
clasp my beloved sailing boat,
then mildly set it on course
for the tropical flannel island.

As we cruise, I lose myself
in my watery paradise,
amid whales, sharks, flying fish..
adventuring will last forever…
I wish…

Have you got your towel,
Philipp?

?

Questions, questions: Who?
What? Why?
We spend so much energy
filling children's heads with
facts and figures as they
grow.
Yet deep inside their heads
lies untold curiosity which
will educate them subtly
and teach them what they
want to know.

Questions, questions,
Why is milk white?
Who painted rainbows?
Why is the moon half-round?
Why do ships float?
What holds up a plane?
So interesting.
So profound.

DOUBT

Everyone has an opinion
on how to rear children aright.
Broadcasters, journalists,
paediatricians, politicians,
offer parents their muddled insight.

Advice to parents is a growth area
'be in charge' – or should we be 'mates'?
Behaviour is simply 'a phase'
'just his age', he'll grow out of it
at varying rates.

'Time out' is a modern stratagem
(in my day it was 'go to your room!')
Now actions produce a reaction
(it used to be ripples in pools).
Professionals and government are grasping the power
and making the parents feel fools.

Such confusion never existed before
as 'parenting' is quite a new thing.
Before the Great War and the ed. psychs,
the therapists, counsellors and the rest,
It used to be 'I'll tell your Father'
and ultimately 'Mother knows best'.

LIFE'S NOT THAT SIMPLE

The teacher talked of global warming
'We've made it all too hot,
our cars, our planes and mobile phones
are causing a melting pot'.

'Miss, why don't they just switch off the lot?'

We watched a film on Africa
where disease causes death and despair.
This girl of twelve cared for a family of five.
Life is so desperate there.

'Miss, why can't we just send her the fare?'

My teacher said life is not simple like that.
There are reasons of justice and cost.
It is not just reaction or feelings inside.
The cutting of trees and the melting of frost
must be argued, sometimes won, sometimes lost.

It turns out her husband's a soldier at war,
he fought for us all in Iraq.
It's all about freedom for people oppressed
and setting democracy on track.
But when we put this to our teacher in class
she just smiled and said 'I want him back!'

TO MY CREDIT...

The Bank of England
has just increased its rate.
Oil prices are on the rise –
problems in Kuwait.
Russia may close the pipeline with Kurdistan –
so gas prices now go higher.
The only thing that stays the same
is my salary – unattainable
that figure to which I would aspire.

How can I direct my children
towards a job that yields a fistful?
Something in the City? A plumber?
An electrician or an international footballer?
it makes me wistful.

But what are their talents?
Financial, technical, physical,
literary, technological, musical?
All we can do is vary their experience.

Perhaps Nursery was right.
The cutting and the sticking
was the preamble for the long fight.

Why do they have to do it all?
Why can't we let them be?
As they develop through the years
it's easier to see.

BEGINNINGS AND ENDINGS

The folder and packed-lunch box,
the blazer proudly worn.
He's eager to be through the gate,
but how my heart is torn.

When first-born started off to school,
it seemed a great relief.
But the speed at which the last one leaves
is fast beyond belief.

The nappies and the buggy
were last week's aggravations.
The baby into toddler into schoolboy
is reality now, not imagination.

All the children off to school,
a chance to be quite free.
Nursery mornings saw the basics done
but little time for me.

Yet now the moment has arrived.
My youngest makes a start.
My baby has gone from before my eyes,
but forever in my heart.

A WORK OF GENERATIONS

Grandma did the poems.
Us three did the art.
Katy did the typing
And Mummy the telling-off part.

'Off to bed at once' she said
'Straight away, you go!'
She thought we were asleep,
but little did she know.

Midnight feasts of ink and pen,
laughter and lots of fun
produced this work of generations
to be enjoyed by everyone.